6/04

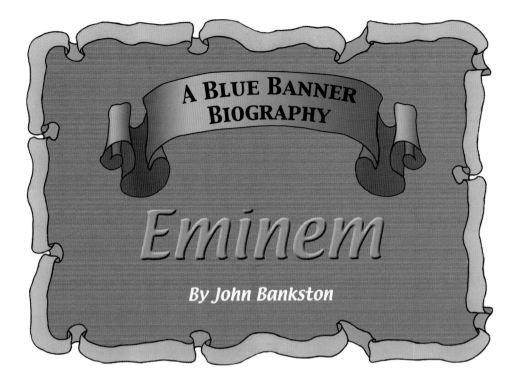

A BLUE BANNER
BIOGRAPHY

Eminem

By John Bankston

YA B EMINEM BAN
Bankston, John
Eminem

$16.95
NEWHOPE   31994011720304

Mitchell Lane
PUBLISHERS

P.O. Box 196
Hockessin, Delaware 19711
Visit us on the web: www.mitchelllane.com
Comments? email us: mitchelllane@mitchelllane.com

Mitchell Lane
PUBLISHERS

Printing   2   3   4   5   6   7   8   9

Blue Banner Biographies

Eminem	Sally Field	Jodie Foster
Melissa Gilbert	Rudy Giuliani	Ron Howard
Michael Jackson	Nelly	Mary-Kate and Ashley Olsen
Daniel Radcliffe	Shirley Temple	Richie Valens
Rita Williams-Garcia	Ja Rule	Jay Z
Missy Elliott	Bow Wow	

Library of Congress Cataloging-in-Publication Data
Bankston, John, 1974-
        Eminem / John Bankston.
            p. cm. -- (Blue banner biography)
Summary: A biography of rap artist Eminem.
Includes bibliographical references (p.   ), discography (p.   ), filmography (p.   ), and index.
        ISBN 1-58415-222-2 (lib. bdg.)
    1. Eminem (Musician)--Juvenile literature. 2. Rap musicians--United States--Biography--Juvenile literature. [1. Eminem (Musician) 2. Musicians. 3. Rap (Music)] I. Title. II. Series.
        ML3930.E46B36 2003
        782.421649'092--dc21
                                                                                    2003004650

ABOUT THE AUTHOR: Born in Boston, Massachusetts, John Bankston has written over three dozen biographies for young adults profiling scientists like Jonas Salk and Alexander Fleming, celebrities like Mandy Moore and Alicia Keys, great achievers like Alfred Nobel, and master musicians like Franz Peter Schubert. He has worked in Los Angeles, California as a producer, screenwriter and actor. Currently he is in pre-production on *Dancing at the Edge*, a semi-autobiographical film he hopes to film in Portland, Oregon. Last year he completed his first young adult novel, *18 to Look Younger*.
PHOTO CREDITS: Cover: AP Photo/Mark J. Terrill; p. 4 Myrna Suarez/Globe Photos, Inc.; p. 12, Bill Pugliano/Getty Images; p. 14 AP Photo/POOL, Denis Doyle; p. 21 Mark Allan/Alpha/Globe Photos, Inc.; p. 25 AP Photo/Kevork Djansezian; p. 27 Globe Photos, Inc.; p. 28 Frank Micelotta/Getty Images
ACKNOWLEDGMENTS: The following story has been thoroughly researched, and to the best of our knowledge, represents a true story. While every possible effort has been made to ensure accuracy, the publisher will not assume liability for damages caused by inaccuracies in the data, and makes no warranty on the accuracy of the information contained herein. This story has not been authorized nor endorsed by Marshall Mathers III (Eminem).

CONTENTS

Growing up with a single mother who moved frequently, Marshall Mathers III was told by most of the people in his life that he'd wind up a failure. He refused to listen. Today he's one of the most successful recording artists in the music business.

"Cleanin' Out My Closet"

No one expected Marshall to be any good. He was used to that. As he and his best friend Proof strode into the cafeteria at Osborne High School, he could feel the students' eyes on him. He didn't go to the school. He was a white kid entering the unfamiliar lunchroom of a predominantly African-American school in inner-city Detroit, and he had every right to be nervous. After all, he wasn't there to pick up an extra course, and he wasn't interested in the day's lunch special.

Marshall Mathers III was there to battle.

The young teen had a gift. In regular life he could be shy and nervous, but when he started to rap, everything changed. He was able to construct bizarre rhymes that seemed to come out of nowhere. Sometimes they were offbeat, sometimes they were off-color, but his skills were sharper than any of the kids' at Osborne, no matter what their race.

"It was like *White Men Can't Jump*," Proof later told *Rolling Stone,* referring to the 1992 basketball film in which Caucasian Woody Harrelson wins his games partly because of his talent and partly because no one expects a white guy to be so skilled. Marshall was the same way, as Proof remembered: "Everybody thought he'd be easy to beat, and they got smoked every time."

At a young age, Marshall realized that was the thing with stereotypes. Sometimes they work against you. Sometimes you figure out a way to make them work for you.

Marshall Mathers would become world famous as Eminem (from his initials M&M), but before he did he'd have to face the same stereotypes over and over again.

Like many hip-hop stars, Marshall grew up poor. "I'm coming from a standpoint where people don't realize there are a lot of poor white people . . . ," he told *The Source* magazine. "No one has a choice where they grow up or what color they are. If you're a rich kid or a ghetto kid you have no control over your circumstances. The only control you have is to get out of your situation or stay in it."

It would be a long time before Marshall would have that type of control over his life. His mother, Debbie, was fifteen years old when she married his dad, twenty-two-

> *Marshall Mathers would have to face stereotypes before he would become world famous as Eminem.*

year-old Marshall Mathers II. Debbie was a singer in her husband's band, the Daddy Warbucks.

Marshall's earliest memories might be musical. When his mother was pregnant with him, she was still performing in the lounges of cheap motels and on the stages of seedy bars along the fringes of the Dakotas and Montana. Neither of Marshall's parents had a future as musicians.

Debbie was seventeen when her son Marshall Bruce Mathers III was born on October 17, 1972, in Kansas City, Missouri. They didn't stay there long.

"We just kept moving back and forth because my mother never had a job," he told *Us Weekly*. "We just kept getting kicked out of every house we were in."

Although she would do everything from working in a beauty salon to running a limo service, money was always tight. Marshall II would take off for days, even weeks at a time, and Debbie was forced to rely on welfare and whatever family help she could muster.

Before Marshall III was out of diapers, his father left unexpectedly for California. He didn't come back. There was no child support, no birthday cards. When Marshall tried to write to his dad, the letters came back unopened, the envelopes marked Return to Sender. Only when he was older and famous would his father try to get in touch

> *Before Marshall was out of diapers, his father left unexpectedly for California. He didn't come back.*

with him. By then it was too late. Marshall wasn't interested in communicating with him.

Still, as an adult artist he'd learn to share the blame. *"When I was just a little baby boy, my momma used to tell me these crazy things. She used to tell me my daddy was an evil man, she used to tell me he hated me,"* he raps on the song "Kill You." *"But then I got a little bit older and I realized she was the crazy one. But there was nothin' I could do or say to try to change her, cuz that's just the way she was."*

Young Marshall had plenty to be angry about. Although his mother has said he exaggerated how tough their life was, even she doesn't deny the frequent moves and job changes. Every few months there would be a new home, and once he was six or seven, a new school. Each new school brought new rules, new cliques, and old problems.

As a kid Marshall was often harassed by bullies. The worst incident he later graphically described in the song "Brain Damage." As a fourth-grader, Marshall was crossing the playground when a sixth-grader "came running across the yard and hit me so hard into a snow bank that I blacked out," he later told *Rolling Stone*. Marshall wound up in a hospital, and as his mother recalled in the same article, "He had a cerebral hemorrhage and was in and out of consciousness for five

Every few months Marshall had a new home and a new school to attend. He was often harassed by bullies.

days. The doctors had given up on him, but I wouldn't give up on my son."

In 1986 Debbie gave birth to another son, Marshall's half brother Nathan. Around the same time, when Marshall was twelve, the family settled in East Detroit, Michigan. A hardscrabble area far from exclusive neighborhoods like Grosse Point, 8 Mile Road formed the area's geographic and cultural boundary. It divided upper- and middle-class neighborhoods from those of the poor and working class. It was a street littered with bars and liquor stores.

School wasn't much better. Marshall was one of the few white kids attending predominantly African-American Lincoln Junior High. Navigating yet another challenge might have been overwhelming, except by then Marshall had found an escape. When he was nine, his uncle Ronnie Polkinghorn introduced him to hip-hop music through the *Breakin'* sound track. Soon he had picked up all the hip-hop he could find, particularly by groups like the Beastie Boys and N.W.A.

When Marshall was nine, his uncle Ronnie Polkinghorn introduced him to hip-hop music.

"Growing up I was one of the biggest fans of N.W.A., from putting on sunglasses and looking in the mirror and lip-synching to wanting to be Dr. Dre, to be Ice Cube," Eminem told *Rolling Stone*. In the late eighties as Marshall was attending high school, their style of hip-hop, often called gangsta rap, was gaining popularity.

Fueled by the rage of the inner city, groups like N.W.A., along with artists like Ice-T, crafted lyrics describing feelings of hopelessness and anger along with verbal attacks on everyone from corrupt police to insecure women. They had an authenticity Marshall couldn't find in other types of music. The lyrics also scared parents and authority figures—which made them even more appealing.

In the lunchroom, Marshall began joining in the rapping contests of his schoolmates. These improvised "battles" were like ghetto word games, relying on speed and skill—a quick mind and a fluid vocabulary. Marshall was well prepared. After long hours in his room pretending he was someone else, Marshall began to get respect as Marshall.

His social life was improving, but school was still next to impossible. He began skipping school and failing classes. At the end of ninth grade he realized he'd flunked. He'd have to repeat freshman year. It was terrible news, but Marshall was about meet his muse—a young woman who would inspire his music.

> **Marshall began skipping school and failing classes. He had to repeat his freshman year.**

"Kim"

Marshall Mathers's second year as a freshman at Lincoln Junior High wasn't much easier than the first. Only one thing made it tolerable.

He fell in love.

Kim Scott was a pretty blond freshman, a few years younger than Marshall but twice as worldly. According to his mother, she came with her share of problems.

"She moved in when she was thirteen," Debbie Mathers-Briggs claimed in an *Us Weekly* interview. "Marshall said she had nowhere else to go. She would have awful tantrums; she just wanted Marshall's attention all the time. There was always jealousy."

If Marshall's life was stressful during his first freshman year, it got worse when he repeated the grade. On his third try as a freshman, he gave up. After dropping out in his mid-teens, Marshall remembers his mother treating him as an adult.

"As soon as I turned fifteen, she was like, 'Get a . . . job and help me with these bills or your [butt] is out,'" he told *Rolling Stone*.

Without a high school diploma, Marshall was only able to land minimum-wage jobs. He was fired frequently, usually for insubordination. He later described these experiences in the song "If I Had . . .": *"I'm tired of jobs startin' off at five fifty an hour then this boss wonders why I'm smartin' off."* He worked at a pizza place and at a gas station. His longest job was at Gilbert's Lodge, a family-style restaurant where he worked as a cook and sometimes got in trouble for rapping the orders.

A source of both inspiration and frustration, Kim Scott has been a major part of Marshall's life for over a decade. She's the mother of his daughter Haile, but they've seen more than their share of problems in their relationship.

Lunchroom battles gave way to open mike nights at the Hip Hop Shop. Marshall competed nearly every Saturday night, and he was usually the only white competitor. In the beginning the audience wasn't too happy to see him and he could barely make himself heard. "As soon as I grabbed the mike I'd get booed," Marshall confessed to *Rolling Stone.* It took a few tries before he got confident enough to own the stage and make sure they listened. Eventually he proved himself to the Hip Hop Shop audiences the same way he'd proved himself at Osborne.

By then Marshall was in his early twenties. He knew he had to make a move. Guys four, five years younger were releasing CDs and becoming successful. Just a few years before, his uncle Ronnie had told him to abandon his hiphop ambitions. Then in late 1993, Ronnie killed himself. His uncle's suicide devastated Marshall, but it also taught him an important lesson. Life was short, and he had to make his time count.

With the backing of a pair of local promoters who'd started independent record label FBT, he began work on his debut, which he called *Infinite.*

Marshall competed at the Hip Hop Shop on open mike nights every Saturday, and he was usually the only white competitor.

Marshall's dreams *were* infinite, and working on the CD made him feel like they might actually come true. Then his girlfriend dropped a bombshell. She was pregnant.

In the beginning of his career, Marshall performed in predominantly African-American clubs. Often he was booed before he picked up the mic. Today his millions of fans include people of every race.

Realizing he was about to be a father increased the pressure tremendously. "It was right before my daughter was born," Marshall told *Rolling Stone*. "So having a future for her was all I talked about." Maybe that's why he decided not to take any chances with his first recording.

Marshall knew he didn't sound like the other rappers he heard at the Hip Hop Shop and on the radio. He worried this would hold him back. He decided in order to succeed he needed to change his sound. Instead of sounding like Eminem, his first CD sounded like a Jay-Z album.

Haile Jade Mathers arrived on Christmas Day, 1995. Marshall was a father. The next year his debut CD was released. It didn't take long for him to realize that trying to sound like everyone else was a bad idea. Radio deejays wouldn't play *Infinite,* and kids didn't buy it. Why should they? There was nothing different about it, there were dozens of rappers who sounded just like him—and they had more money for production values, that lush combination of instrumentation and background vocals that sets apart expensive, major-record-label releases from independents like FBT.

Marshall wound up with cases of unsold CDs. He was forced to sell them from the trunk of his car.

Just as humiliating, only a few days before his daughter's first birthday, Marshall was fired from Gilbert's Lodge. He had forty dollars to his name. He and Kim were fighting. Marshall felt consumed by rage and pain. But in 1997 all his rage, all his pain, would flow into a character. That character would make Eminem world famous and just as threatening to most parents as the gangsta rap he'd loved as a kid.

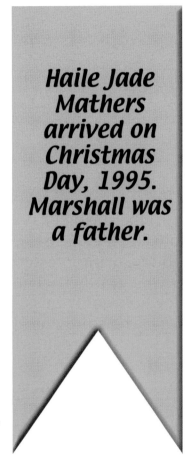

Haile Jade Mathers arrived on Christmas Day, 1995. Marshall was a father.

"My Name Is"

*I*n the spring of 1997, life in the Mathers household looked bleak. Kim and Marshall moved into a crime-ridden, drug-infested neighborhood. One night Kim was washing dishes when a bullet exploded through the window, narrowly missing her before burying itself in the wall. The family had been "adopted" by one of the local addicts, who regularly broke in and stole things to pawn for drug money. "I went through four TVs and five VCRs in two years," Kim later told *Rolling Stone*.

But when Marshall, Kim, and baby Haile moved in with Marshall's mother, life got worse. He claimed his mother was beset by mood swings brought on by prescription drug abuse, a charge she denies, telling *Us Weekly* that the only drugs she took were prescribed for injuries after she was hit by a drunk driver. "I was a total mess," she said. "I couldn't swallow solid foods."

Every aspect of Marshall's life seemed headed in the exact opposite direction of his dreams. It was then he created Slim Shady. Shady was Marshall's alter ego—a character who could act exactly the opposite of the way people are supposed to act.

"I had this whole Slim Shady concept of being two different people, two different sides of me," Marshall was quoted on the Internet Movie Database Web site (IMDb.com) and on planet-eminem.com. "One of them I was tryin' to let go and I looked at the mirror and smashed it. That was the whole intro of *The Slim Shady EP*. Slim Shady was coming to haunt me, was coming to haunt Eminem."

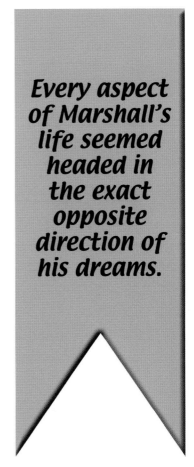

Every aspect of Marshall's life seemed headed in the exact opposite direction of his dreams.

Marshall had learned something from the disappointing sales of *Infinite.* "I had nothing to lose but something to gain," he has said. "If I made an album for me and it was to my satisfaction, then I succeeded. If I didn't, then my producers were going to give up on the whole rap thing."

The anger he felt toward his mother and toward the low-paying, humiliating jobs he'd held well into his twenties, Marshall poured into his music. He scribbled lyrics on scraps of paper in handwriting so small no one else could read them. Writing was therapy. He described his problems with Kim, with his mother, and with a city so decaying that parts of it were set ablaze every October on Devils Night (the night before Halloween).

The eight-song *Slim Shady EP* was honest, real, and frightening. But without any major label backing it, the collection faced the same fate as *Infinite.* His first collection was ignored for its content, but Marshall worried that his second CD was being ignored because of his color. As Dr. Dre later told *Rolling Stone,* "It's like seeing a black guy doing country and western."

Marshall was haunted by the legacy of one white rap artist in particular. When Marshall was a teenager, the rapper Vanilla Ice topped the Billboard charts. He sold millions of albums. He became famous. Because he lied about his upbringing, he also guaranteed that solo white hip-hop acts would be totally ignored for nearly a decade.

Being compared to Vanilla Ice was just about the worst insult Marshall could imagine. To him it was never a matter of color. It was a matter of skills. And he was about to prove he had them.

In Detroit his open mike wins and *The Slim Shady EP* were slowly gaining Marshall enough of a following to be approached by Paul "Bunyan" Rosenberg, a local lawyer who wanted to manage Marshall's career. Marshall wondered exactly what career Rosenberg would be managing, but he had nothing to lose.

Not long after, Rosenberg arranged for Marshall to compete in the Rap Olympics in Los Angeles. The top

Marshall's manager arranged for him to compete in the Rap Olympics in Los Angeles.

prize was $1,500. It couldn't have come at a better time. He and Kim were on the outs and Marshall had moved into his own place. Unfortunately, right before he left for L.A., he was evicted. The night before his flight, Marshall broke into the apartment and slept on the floor. There was no heat, no electricity. The situation just fed fuel into his fire.

"Give it to the white boy," an audience member yelled the moment Marshall finished his first set in Los Angeles. Rosenberg agreed, but the judges didn't. After surviving round after round, Marshall came in second. He was furious. As far as he was concerned, number two was failure. What he didn't notice was the small group of record executives huddled around his new manager.

They didn't care that Eminem had come in number two. As far as they were concerned, he was on his way to being number one.

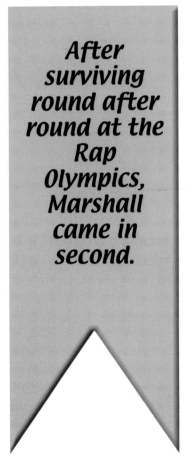

After surviving round after round at the Rap Olympics, Marshall came in second.

CHAPTER 4

"The Eminem Show"

"He really looked like he was going to cry," Marshall Mathers's manager, Paul Rosenberg, admitted to *Rolling Stone*, recalling the day his client came in second at Los Angeles's Rap Olympics. Home in Detroit, Marshall had no money and no place to live, and suddenly it looked like life in L.A. wasn't going to be any better.

Marshall was wrong.

During an appearance on radio station Power 106, Marshall began freestylin'. Dr. Dre was listening. Andre "Dr. Dre" Young was a former member of N.W.A. and a current top producer who'd impressed critics producing Snoop Dogg's debut CD *Doggy Style.* By 1997, Dre was president of Aftermath Records, a division of the major label Interscope. He was listening to the radio when Eminem was introduced.

Dre wanted to hear more. This was easily done — it was Interscope executives who'd approached Rosenberg after Marshall's second-place finish at the Rap Olympics. *The Slim Shady EP* was waiting for Dre when he went into the office.

"In my entire career in the music industry," Dr. Dre told *Rolling Stone,* "I have never found anything from a demo tape or a CD. When Jimmy [Iovine, president of Interscope] played this, I said, 'Find him. Now.'"

Marshall was still in Los Angeles.

Instead of going back to Detroit, he went into the studio, recording with the man he considered his hero. He recorded four songs the first day in the studio—an incredible amount of work. Many of the songs from *The*

Slim Shady allowed Marshall to express a darker side of his creativity. Here he performs with Dr. Dre, who signed him to Aftermath Records and allowed him to reach a larger audience.

Slim Shady EP appeared on this new project, *The Slim Shady LP*, but Dre added his own touch—a higher quality of sound, better instrumentation, and even vocal tracks. More than just a better sound, Dr. Dre gave the project something Marshall could never have given it on his own: credibility.

> **Over one million copies of The Slim Shady LP were shipped the first month.**

With Dre's participation, Eminem, Slim Shady, and Marshall Mathers were featured in top hip-hop publications like *Vibe* and *The Source,* along with main-stream music magazines like *Rolling Stone* and *Spin.* All of this happened long before February 1999, when his first video hit MTV and his music hit the stores.

Over one million copies of the CD were shipped the first month, an unprecedented level for an artist completely unknown just a year before. They quickly sold, and more CDs were pressed.

In many ways it looked like all of the problems, all of the pain, were in the rearview mirror.

"Me rappin' about ... bein' broke and this and that, it's like a pun on the album," Marshall told London's *Melody Maker* magazine. "It's like, my family and people around me always told me that I would grow up to be nothing and my teachers in school and everyone said it. I dropped out of high school, I failed ninth grade three times, I couldn't keep a job, people said that I wouldn't amount to anything. And I portray myself as the biggest loser in the world. . . . Look at me now."

The whole world was looking—and not everyone liked what they saw. For every fan like the one quoted in *Teen People* who gave Eminem props because "the things he raps about are real," there was another like Vermonter Hannah Van Sustern, who complained, "Artists should have respect for one another whether or not they get along and Eminem does not."

As controversial as his lyrics were to teens, it was their effect on adults that got the most press. Conservatives like Linda Cheney, wife of Vice President Dick Cheney, attacked them for being obscene. But to some it was the liberal backlash from groups that usually championed freedom of speech that was most surprising. Gay & Lesbian Advocates & Defenders, or GLAD, which champions legal rights for gays and lesbians, attacked what they considered antigay lyrics, while women's rights groups like NOW attacked what they viewed as anti-woman lyrics. Even fellow recording artists spoke out against Marshall's lyrics. Techno musician Moby said at the 2000 Grammy Awards, "I was talking to somebody about the notion of Eminem [being] like Elvis Presley, The Sex Pistols and Kurt Cobain. The difference is they were rebellious in that they were expanding boundaries. Eminem is creating a culture that appeals to the lowest common denominator."

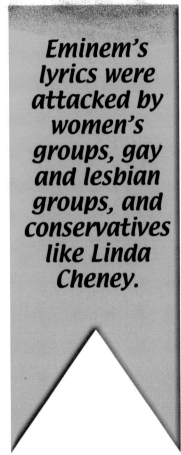

Eminem's lyrics were attacked by women's groups, gay and lesbian groups, and conservatives like Linda Cheney.

Marshall was even attacked by Timothy White, the editor in chief of *Billboard* magazine, the recording industry's trade journal. White accused Eminem of "making money by exploiting the world's misery."

While Marshall would have lyrical follow-ups to Cheney and Moby in his 2002 CD *The Eminem Show,* sales of *The Slim Shady LP* (over 8 million in the United States alone) eased the pain. Attacks by family members were tougher to deal with.

In September 1999, Marshall's mother Debbie Mathers-Briggs sued him, saying in her claim that he had made "defaming comments about her . . . including descriptions of her as pill-popping and lawsuit happy." In response, Rosenberg issued a statement, saying, "Everything he said can be verified as true."

His mother would also release her own CD disputing her son's claims. The album did not sell well. In an interview with *US Magazine,* she said when Marshall's half brother Nathan "gets out there he will do better [as a rapper]." In the end, Marshall's mother settled for $25,000, a tiny fraction of the $10 million she'd originally sought.

In 2000, Marshall's biggest problems weren't with his mother, but with the mother of his child. He and Kim married on June 14, 1999, but they were far from happily

> *In 2000, Marshall and his wife Kim encountered many problems in their relationship, and in October 2001, they divorced.*

married. They separated several times. In June 2000 Marshall spied Kim at a local bar, kissing construction worker John Guerra. A fight ensued in which Marshall hit Guerra with an unloaded pistol. The next month while Marshall was touring, Kim tried to kill herself. (Nathan found her, and her injuries turned out to be minor). Their relationship battles continued through 2001, overshadowing Marshall's triumphs, which included multiple Grammy nominations and performing a duet of "Stan" with openly gay recording artist Elton John.

In October 2001, Kim and Marshall divorced. By then he was embarking on a brand-new career.

Although many members of the gay community were threatened by Marshall's lyrics, his work was championed by openly gay recording artist, Elton John. The two very different artists performed a duet of Marshall's hit "Stan" at the Grammy Awards on February 21, 2001.

"Lose Yourself"

*T*hroughout his career, Marshall couldn't completely shake Vanilla's Ice's embarrassing legacy. In the winter of 2001, he risked following the failed hip-hop star's path into oblivion.

Cool As Ice was designed to create a movie star from Robert Van Winkle—Vanilla Ice's real name. Released by Universal Pictures in 1991, it came out while his music sales slowed and revelations about his background surfaced. Winkle didn't grow up in a tough part of Miami, as he'd claimed, he'd grown up affluent in an upper-middle-class neighborhood in Dallas. "I was just trying to keep people from messing with my family," he told reporters at the time.

Not only was the movie poorly written and directed, but Vanilla's performance was so laughable it turned a drama into camp comedy. Its fate was Marshall's worst nightmare.

Hip-hop artists have successfully crossed over from music to film for over a decade. LL Cool J and Ice-T earn more money as actors now than they do as recording artists, while Ice Cube not only acts but produces, writes, and directs. These were Marshall's ambitions as well.

None of the others, though, took the huge risk of starring in a movie based on his own life.

"I always felt like I had some natural ability to act," he told *Spin* magazine, "but this wasn't a little cameo or something—I had to carry the whole movie."

The pressure was as great as any he'd felt as a rapper. Marshall applied the lessons he'd learned from his music. *Infinite* was made with little money by unknown producers. *The Slim Shady LP* had major money behind it and the talents of top producer Dr. Dre.

For his movie star debut, Marshall didn't want low-budget, inexperienced filmmakers. The movie would be

Opposite respected actor Mekhi Phifer, Marshall was widely praised for his honest performance in 8 Mile.

Movie star and platinum selling hip-hop star, Marshall Mathers won two Grammy Awards on February 23, 2003. Still, for Marshall the most important prize is the love and respect of his daughter, Haile.

produced by Imagine Entertainment, the company co-owned by Ron Howard and responsible for blockbusters like *How The Grinch Stole Christmas* and intellectual fare like *A Beautiful Mind.* The director, Curtis Hanson, had received critical acclaim for *L.A. Confidential* and *The Wonder Boys.* Marshall didn't just come up with the idea of doing a movie about hip-hop. The filmmakers had been considering one for months.

"We were trying to tell a story about the fans of hip-hop," Hanson told *Spin.* "The power, the meaning that it had in their lives, but also the dream that success in hip-hop represents. In another era it could be basketball or boxing."

Although Marshall had never acted before, both Hanson and producer Brian Grazer were impressed with what they saw of him on his videos and in awards shows. They could tell he had range — the ability to show a variety of emotions. Still, casting Marshall in *8 Mile* was a big gamble.

The gamble paid off. The film impressed critics and fans. It would earn over $100 million.

Marshall Mathers is in his thirties now, and his time as a top hip-hop artist may be limited. As a critic reviewing *The Eminem Show* pointed out, Marshall may be the only man his age who can name all the members of 'N Sync. Calling out to Moby, "He's too old, it's over," when the techno artist has less than half a dozen years on him just shows how brief a recording artist's career can be. It can be tough for a man in his thirties to emotionally connect with teenage music fans.

Marshall's acting debut in the film *8 Mile* impressed critics and fans. The film earned over $100 million.

Yet his acting debut's critical and box office response may prove he has a future in film. For now, he's comfortable being daddy to Haile, telling *People* magazine, "My daughter is growing up and I'm trying to set an example for her." One example may be welcoming her mother back into his life. In late 2002, Kim moved back into the mansion he now owns, far from the grime and crime of 8 Mile Road. She brought with her a five-month-old baby, conceived while the two were separated. For Marshall Mathers, the real-life Eminem Show continues.

CHRONOLOGY

1972 Marshall Bruce "Eminem" Mathers III is born on October 17 in Kansas City, Missouri

1984 moves with mother Debbie Mathers to East Detroit, Michigan

1989 drops out of high school while repeating ninth grade for the third time

1995 daughter Haile Jade is born on Christmas Day

1996 releases his debut album *Infinite;* it sells poorly

1997 completes *The Slim Shady EP* on his own; finishes second in Los Angeles's Annual Rap Olympics; Dr. Dre produces *The Slim Shady LP*

1999 *The Slim Shady LP* is released—it will sell over 8 million copies; marries Kim Scott

2000 is accused of pistol-whipping John Guerra, a man he sees kissing Kim

2001 divorces Kim

2002 is sentenced to probation for assault against Guerra, and he agrees to pay him $100,000; Film *8 Mile* is released—it will earn over $100 million

2003 wins two Grammy Awards, for Best Rap Album *(The Eminem Show)* and for Best Short Form Music Video ("Without Me"); wins Academy Award for Original Song, "Lose Yourself"

DISCOGRAPHY

1996	Infinite
1998	*The Slim Shady EP*
1999	*The Slim Shady LP*
2000	*The Marshall Mathers LP*
2002	*The Eminem Show*
2002	*8 Mile* (sound track)

Selected Awards

1999   MTV Video Music Award (VMA) — Best New Artist — "My Name Is"
Grammy Award for Best Rap Solo Performance — "My Name Is"
Grammy Award for Best Rap Album — *The Slim Shady LP*

2000   MTV VMA — Best Video of the Year — "The Real Slim Shady"
MTV VMA — Best Rap Video — "Forgot About Dre"
MTV VMA — Best Male in a Video — "The Real Slim Shady"
Source Award for Best Video of the Year — "Guilty Conscience"
Source Award for Best Lyricist of the Year

2001   Source Award for Best Video of the Year — "Stan"
Billboard Music Award — Best Maximum Vision Clip of the Year — "The Real Slim Shady"
Billboard Music Award — Best Rap/Hip Hop Clip of the Year — "The Real Slim Shady"
Grammy Award — Best Rap Album of the Year — *The Marshall Mathers LP*
Grammy Award — Best Rap Duo or Group — "Forgot About Dre"
Grammy for Best Rap Solo Performance — "The Real Slim Shady"

2002   Billboard Music Award for Best Album — *The Eminem Show*
Billboard Music Award — Best R&B/Hip Hop Album — *The Eminem Show*
MTV VMA for Best Video of the Year — "Without Me"
MTV VMA for Best Male Video — "Without Me"
MTV VMA for Best Rap Video — "Without Me"
MTV VMA for Best Direction in a Video — "Without Me"

2003   Grammy Award for Best Rap Album — *The Eminem Show*
Grammy Award for Best Short Form Music Video — "Without Me"
American Music Award for Album, Hip Hop/R&B — *The Eminem Show*
American Music Award for Album, Pop/Rock 'n Roll — *The Eminem Show*
American Music Award for Favorite Male Artist, Pop/Rock 'n Roll
American Music Award for Favorite Male Artist, Hip Hop/R&B
Academy Award for Best Original Song — "Lose Yourself"

FOR FURTHER READING

Gigney, Scott, and Harper, Mann. *His Name Is: The Eminem Story in Words and Pictures.* London: Chrome Dreams, 2001.

Gittins, Ian. *Eminem.* New York: Carlton Press, 2001.

Huxley, Martin. *Eminem.* New York: Griffin Trade Paperback, 2000.

Mander, Hannah. *Access All Areas: Eminem.* London: Michael O'Mara Books, 2002.

On the Internet:

Eminem.com

Eminemworld.com

INDEX